I Carry my Ancestors in my Bones

A Love Letter to Every Version of Me

davina@alegriamagazine.com

ISBN: 979-8-9945494-2-1
Published by: Alegria Publishing
Original Illustration by: Soni Lopez-Chavez
Book cover and layout by: @mckadamia

I CARRY MY ANCESTORS IN MY BONES

A Love Letter to Every Version of Me

Poems by
HORTENCIA JIMÉNEZ, PH.D

ALEGRÍA
PUBLISHING

I dedicate this poetry book to my three children and to everyone walking the path of healing. To those nurturing their inner child, their younger selves, and the person they are becoming. May these poems bring comfort, connection, and the reminder that you are not alone.

Preface

I wrote this poetry book during a season of my life filled with pain, grief, sadness, and deep transformation. It was my therapist who first suggested that I put my pain into words, who encouraged me to transmute everything I was holding into language, into art.

This collection is vulnerable, raw, and deeply authentic, an intimate invitation into my soul. It feels scary to reveal so much of my thoughts and feelings publicly, but I know that someone out there will resonate with these poems, especially mujeres who are healing their inner *niña*. I trust that my words will touch your heart, help you feel seen, remind you that you are not alone, and affirm that your story matters.

This book is an offering for anyone on a healing journey, for anyone longing to feel understood, held, and validated. It is an invitation back to your truest, most liberated self.

Fifty percent of this book's proceeds will be donated to the Mariposa Rising Scholarship, an endowed scholarship for undocumented students transferring from Hartnell College to the university. Transforming pain into poetry and returning it to the community is part of how healing becomes collective.

Con mucho cariño, amor, y gratitud,
Dra. Hortencia Jiménez

Forward

I first discovered poetry when I was sixteen. The world around me was falling apart, and poetry gave me language for what I was living through. It helped me name the conditions around me— poverty, fear, longing, displacement. Poetry became a place where I could tell the truth. It became a way to survive.

In this collection, we witness Dr. Hortencia Jiménez doing that same work: naming what she carries. These poems are honest and unguarded. They move through memory, grief, joy, and endurance without trying to clean anything up. This is not a book that looks away. It stays with the hard things long enough for them to speak.

Jiménez invites us into the most personal parts of her life, and in doing so, creates space for our own stories to surface. As readers, we sit with her emotions—the tenderness, the anger, the love—and we begin to recognize ourselves in them. That recognition matters. It reminds us that our experiences are not isolated, and that our feelings make sense in the context of the lives we've lived.

Poetry is an exchange. The writer offers the work, and the reader brings their own history to the page. These poems will likely activate memories you didn't expect, moments you thought you had moved past. That activation is not accidental—it is how empathy is built, how connection happens. This book is a guide to finding yourself by paying attention. It asks you to show up as you are, without shrinking or editing yourself. It invites you to imagine a world—and a life—where all parts of you are allowed to exist, fully and without apology.

Yosimar Reyes-Santa Clara County Poet Laureate and 2024 Creative Ambassador by the City of San José.

Table of Contents

SECTION 2 ROOTS AND MEMORY:
LA TIERRA EN MIS HUESOS

Section 1
Inner Niña Wounds

Abandoned

Abandoned.
A word that cuts deep,
harsher than it sounds.

I know I'm not the only one
who carries its echo.
I was a child
when my father left for this country,
promising reunion in Mexico,
with my mother, and my sisters.

But he did not take me.
He left me behind,
with my grandmother and aunt,
a small child learning
what absence feels like.

Abandonment became my
shadow, my friend, my wisdom.
A quiet companion I did not choose.
I have made peace with it,
but the ache still hurts.
Because healing doesn't erase,
it teaches us to breathe around the wound.

And I've learned as an adult that
we abandon ourselves too.
At work.
In love.
In friendships.
In remaining calladita,
in shrinking our bodies
so we don't take up space.
In postponing or ending
our dreams and aspirations
por la familia.
In trying to fit into
societal standards
that were never meant for us.

We leave behind
our truest selves, our authenticity
our voices,
our colors,
everything that makes us unique,
just to be accepted.

But I am here to tell you
that you do not need to abandon yourself.
Speak your truth,
even with a trembling, chillona voice.
Even when your passion and anger shakes the room.

Be your authentic self,
even when it makes others uncomfortable.

Don't believe the toxic BS.
You are not unlovable,
broken,
or damaged
for having been abandoned.

You are love.
You are light.
You are hope.
You are the model
of what is possible
when we transmute our abandoned pain
into love.
Because you were never truly abandoned
if you never left yourself.

Embarrassed

Embarrassed
of my skin color,
my brown rooted origins,
embarrassed for being *del rancho,*
for growing up in the U.S.
without my parents,
raised by legal guardians.

Embarrassed
for coming from a poor,
working-class family,
for working in the fields,
for being undocumented,
for failing kinder
because English was not yet a dominant language.

Embarrassed
for being one of the tallest girls
in elementary school,
for being attracted to girls,
embarrassed of my *trenzas,*
for eating nopales,
for my accent.

I spent years embarrassed
of everything
that made me human,
Everything that made me who I am.

It took my adult self
to return to that inner niña,
to hold her,
to heal,
to unlearn the lies
that taught me to hide and shrink.

You are never too late
to heal,
to embrace
every piece of you.

What once felt like shame
is now my superpower
I love all of me.

When Life Feels Too Heavy

When life feels too heavy,
pause.

Take a breath.
Come back to the present.
Today is a gift,
and that's why it's called the present.

Notice what surrounds you.

What do you see
the colors,
the shapes,
the light?

What do you smell?
Does a scent carry memories,
an aura of comfort,
a reminder of home?

What do you hear
the soft hum
of life moving around you?

What can you touch,
feel,
or hold in your hands?

Tuning into your body and the world around you
in ways that feel accessible to you
is a simple yet profound way
to come home to the present moment

When life feels too heavy,
release the weight of tomorrow.
Don't overthink the future.

Take it one day at a time.
one hour at a time.
one minute at a time.

Overthinking adds layers of stress,
pulling us into pain,
grief,
and sometimes darkness.

When life feels too heavy,
remember
you are loved.

There are people
who care for you,
people who love you,
even when your mind
tells you otherwise.

You are not alone,
even when it feels like it.

When life feels too heavy,
reach out.
Ask for help.

Let someone
carry the weight with you.

Because you were never meant
to carry it all
alone.

Chillona

Soy chillona y chingona

When I Am Struggling Self Love Looks Like

When I am struggling,
self-love looks like
allowing myself to be a *chillona*,
to hold space for my emotions
without judgment.

When I am struggling,
self-love looks like feeling it all
without shame,
without silencing the voice that says,
"*Hortencia, deja de llorar,*
¿por qué eres tan chillona?
Get yourself together."
But instead, whispering back,
it's okay to feel,
it's okay to cry.

When I am struggling,
self-love looks like
tapping into ancestral healing
taking a bath with my herbs,
hacerme una limpia,
tending to my spirit
with love and compassion,
reminding my inner niña
that she is not alone.

I see you, Tenchita.
I know you are sad.
I know you are in pain.
I see you and I honor you.
I hold you in my heart,
te abrazo y te recuerdo que no estás sola.
I am here for you.

When I am struggling,
self-love looks like reaching out,
telling my friends I'm not okay,
that today feels heavy.

When I am struggling,
self-love looks like vulnerability
embracing the *chillona*,
the heart-led Hortencia
who feels deeply.
That is self-love.

The kind of love
that is radical,
tender,
unapologetic
embracing the most fragile
parts of myself
without judgment.

When I am struggling,
self-love looks like doing the basics
brushing my teeth,
washing my face,
taking my vitamins,
drinking water,
eating a meal
Simple things,
but sacred ones.

Self-love is finding
pockets of joy
throughout the day,
even when the light
feels far away.

Tears are Medicine

Tears are medicine.
They bring calm.
They bring peace.
They bring clarity.

Tears are grounding.
They bring you back to yourself.
They are a release.
They are surrender.
They are truth spilling free.

Tears are sacred.
Allow them to flow,
que corran por tu cara,
deja que te acaricien
como un río sagrado
que limpia,
que sana,
que te devuelve a ti.
Tears are medicine

Don't judge your tears.

The Shame I Carry in My Body Does Not Belong to Me

The shame I carry in my body
does not belong to me.
It was planted there
by the Catholic Church,
by *la familia,*
by the women in my life
who were themselves carrying shame
my abuelita, mi tía, mi mamá,
and others who passed down
what had been imposed on them.

It crept in through simple phrases:
"tápate,"
"no andes enseñando,"
"no seas cochina."
"callate, no digas nada"

Words that taught me to shrink,
to stay small,
to silence my voice,
to dilute myself.
And with that,
I lost trust
and confidence
in who I was.

The shame I carry in my body
does not belong to me.

The shame of being molested as a child,
internalizing the threats and warnings
"no vayas a decir nada,"
"quién te va a creer,"
"te van a regañar"

I carried this silence for years
a silence that was never mine to hold.

The shame of being sexually assaulted as a teenager
and losing my virginity to violence.
I was raised in purity culture,
where a woman's worth
was tied to her virginity.

But what happens
when that "purity"
is stolen
through force,
through violence,
through trauma?

The shame told me
I was dirty,
unworthy,
broken,
damaged goods.

Heavy, painful words
but they lived inside me
because of the shame
I inherited.

The shame I carry in my body
does not belong to me.
It never did.

Now,
I am reclaiming my story.
I am reclaiming my inner niña.
I am reclaiming my teenage self,
the one who carried these wounds in silence.

I refuse to stay calladita.
owning my story is power.
speaking it out loud is liberation.

Don't let your abuser,
your family,
or *el qué dirán*
tell you to dim your light.
or to be ashamed
You are powerful.

You are worthy.

We have the power to heal,
to feel safe in our bodies again.

Treat your body with
compassion,
care,
love,
tenderness.

To explore your body
is an act of radical self-love
You already carry
everything within you
to heal.
You are already whole.

I Love You, But I'm Not In Love With You

I love you deeply,
but I am not in love with you.
This has been a hard truth
one that brought me to the edge of despair and
darkness
one that I resisted,
one that still aches.

In the depths of that grief,
I came to realize something sacred.
You will forever be an important part of my life
I love you for who you are
For your values.
For your humanity.
For being exactly who you are
loving, compassionate, patient, empathetic,
supportive.

I love you deeply for honoring me,
for witnessing my change and transformation
over the decades we shared.
For standing beside me as I grew,
for giving me space to spread my wings,
to arrive at horizons I once believed
were unreachable.

I love you deeply,
but I am not in love with you
And that truth cuts deep in my heart.
Because when I said *yes,*
I meant it wholeheartedly.
Until death do us part
But sometimes life,
sometimes Creator,
has a divine plan
we cannot understand
I asked again and again:
Why now? Why us?

I see it clearly now.
You came into my life
to help me be free,
to help me step into my authentic self,
to help liberate me from so much oppression.

You were my supportive partner,
my best friend,
my partner in crime,
eras mi todo,
mi media naranja,
my mirror,
my anchor when I needed grounding and safety.

I love you deeply.

And because of that love,
we created three beautiful children
our greatest legacy,
our eternal bond.
I love you.

I Breathe In... I Breathe Out...

I Breathe In... I Breathe Out...
I breathe in...
I breathe out...
I breathe in life,
full of light and love.
I breathe in hope
that tomorrow holds possibility.
I breathe in hunger
for living fully.
I breathe in
radical surrender.
I breathe in peace
and grounding.
I breathe out fear
and uncertainty.
I breathe out
what no longer serves
my highest good.
I breathe out anxiety.
I breathe out
limiting beliefs.
I breathe out
the weight
I was never meant
to carry.

Lecciones del Corazón

The people who enter your life
are not here to break you,
but to make you stronger,
to teach you lessons.

Lecciones aunque duelan,
lessons that may crack your spirit,
that may bring you to tears,
that may have you questioning,
your worth, your path, your corazón.
But even in the breaking,
there is becoming.
Even in the pain,
there is purpose.
Some people,
some souls arrive
to mirror your wounds,
to show you where healing
still lives in silence
in the shadows.

Others come
to remind you of your Chingona power,
of your strength,
Of your intelligence,
your softness,
your capacity to love again
even after being shattered
and heartbroken.

Not everyone is meant to stay.
Some come for weeks,
months,
years,
or seasons in your life.
But everyone leaves something behind
an experience,
a lesson,
a truth,
a boundary,
a blessing.

Always something
you can grow from.
Something
that helps you learn
a little more
about yourself.

The people who enter your life
are not here to destroy you.
They are here to awaken you,
 to stretch your spirit,
 to return you home
to yourself.

Lecciones del corazón
aunque duelan,
they are sacred invitations
to rise,
to grow,
to remember
who you are.

In Every Heartbreak

In every heartbreak,
I learned to return to myself
to radically honor the woman within,
to choose *me,*
before betraying my spirit,
my values,
my truth.
It is through every heartbreak
that I have become
the woman I am today.

Turn the Pain into Something Beautiful

Turn the pain into something beautiful.
Say it with me,
turn my pain into something beautiful.

Not because pain deserves to be numbed or
dismissed,
but because you deserve relief.

You deserve moments of joy,
because your breath deserves to be more than grief
and sadness,
because your body deserves to rest and remember
joy.

Turn despair into words that bloom on a page.
Let your shovel dig soft holes in the soil
to plant seeds that you will water
and watch grow into flowers, vegetables, and fruits
reminding you of the beauty of birthing and light.

Turn heartbreak into color.
Draw, paint, cook, knit colorful pieces of art
because you are are a living beautiful art piece

Healing is not only about pain.
Healing is about being aware, being present.
It's noticing the light in between the cracks.

It's the smile of a stranger
that finds you when you're not expecting it.
It's the bees, tiny workers doing sacred work
by pollinating the flowers like a prayer.
It's the wind trenzando tu cabello,
the breeze wrapping itself across your body.
It's your dog shaking a toy like it's the first.
It's the rhythm of your caderas
as you take your dog on a neighborhood walk.

Joy does not mute pain.
Joy walks beside it. Son mejores amigas
Both can live here
both can live in you

I know it's not easy to find joy in your pain.
Say it with me:
"Both can live here."
"Both can live in me."
Again,
"Both can live here."
"Both can live in me."

Turn the pain into something beautiful
Repeat it with me.
Turn my pain into something beautiful,
but don't force it.

No tengas prisa
Let it unfold despacito, lentamente y suavecito.
No lo forces.
Don't force joy.

You decide when.
You decide how.
The pace is yours.
The shape and colors is yours.
The story is yours.
The joy is yours.
Your pain is yours.

Maybe today's beauty is sunbathing naked.
Maybe it's washing a dish without collapsing into
tears.
Maybe it's stepping outside and letting the sky
touch your face.
Maybe it's whispering to your inner niña, "I see
you. You are not alone."
Maybe it's a cumbia move unannounced,
and leaves your caderas lighter than before.

Turn the pain into something beautiful.
Say it with me,
turn my pain into something beautiful,
into words that are no longer silent,
Speak your truth mija, that is beautiful.

Turn the pain into something beautiful.
Repeat it with me,
turn my pain into something beautiful,
a poem, a prayer, a meal, a song.
A boundary. A yes. A no.
A body that feels like home again.
A life that blooms in its own terms.

Turn the pain into something beautiful.
Say it with me,
turn my pain into something beautiful,
that brings you healing,
not by muting, dismissing, or erasing your
experiences,
but by honoring what is happening to you.
Right now, your transformation
en tu corazón, en tu espíritu, en tu cuerpo, en tu voz,
en tu ser.

Turn the pain into something beautiful.
Repeat it with me,
turn my pain into something beautiful.
You are still here.
You are still becoming.
You are still releasing.
You are still transmuting.
You are still shedding.
You are transforming.

Because even in the darkest depths of despair,
There is light.
You are light.
You are alive.

Turn the pain into something beautiful!
And let your beauty radiate inward and in the lives
of others

Courage

Courage is fucken messy and painful
- *courage is growing pains.*

Abuelita

Abuelita,
Abuelita, cuánto la quiero
y cuánto la extraño.
Ya casi son tres años desde su partida
y todavía no aprendo
cómo vivir en un mundo
donde no está.

Me hace tanta falta.

Fue una mujer
que no se rajaba,
una mujer que no se daba por vencida.
Aunque la vida le diera chingadazos,
aunque la tumbara una y otra vez,
usted se levantaba.
¡Como chingados no!

Eso me enseño.

No crecí escuchando "te quiero" de sus labios,
no crecí envuelta en caricias ni palabras suaves.
De niña no entendía por qué
De adulta, sí.

A usted no le enseñaron a amar con ternura.
La vida fue dura, cruel,
y la entrenó para sobrevivir,
no para descansar.
Le dio un escudo,
no un lenguaje para el cariño.

No la culpo, Abuelita.
aunque mi niña interior
y mi yo joven
sí necesitaban ese amor,
hoy entiendo
que hizo lo que pudo
con lo que le dieron.

Y aun así, me dio el regalo más grande
ver cómo aprendio a amar distinto
con mis hijos.

Con tus bisnietos,
su amor se volvió visible.
se volvió abrazo, risa, paciencia.
al amarlos a ellos,
me amo a mí
de una forma nueva.

Usted era mi base.
Mi raíz.
Mi árbol de vida.
No la tengo en cuerpo,

pero la siento en espíritu,
en mis decisiones,
en mi fuerza,
en la claridad que llega
en mis días más dolorosos,
más tristes,
en mis momentos más oscuros.

Gracias, Abuelita,
por la fortaleza que corre por mi sangre,
por sus consejos que todavía me sostienen,
por enseñarme a levantarme
cada vez que caigo.

Y para todas las niñas interiores
que crecieron con una Abuelita dura,
con amor fuerte,
con cariño que no siempre supo mostrarse

Tu Abuelita te amó profundamente,
aunque no supiera cómo decirlo

Risks

Take the risks
you've been avoiding
Arriésgate!
No esperes más
The perfect moment
doesn't exist
you create it
with every brave step
you take
Fear will whisper,
"Not yet,"
"No estoy lista"
but your spirit knows
it's time
Arriésgate!
Porque lo que está destinado
para ti
no se encuentra en la zona cómoda
Leap
Trust
You are ready

Mi Tenchita

Mi Tenchita,
hoy quiero decirte
que estoy muy orgullosa de ti
not just for what you've accomplished,
but for who you are.

Por decidir vivir una vida auténtica,
the one you couldn't live
when you were a little girl,
a teenager,
and now, as an adult,
you finally are.

Mi Tenchita,
hoy quiero decirte
que te amo,
que te acepto,
that you are not broken,
you are not damaged goods.
You are *perfectly imperfect.*

Mi Tenchita,
hoy quiero decirte
that everything you went through
was not your fault.
You are not responsible
for the choices
that your *papá*, your *abuelita*,
or your *tía* made.

Mi Tenchita,
te quiero afirmar
que eres amor
that you have always been loved
by your *papás* and *hermanas*,
even when physical borders
separated you from them
You were always,
and still are,
close to their hearts.

Mi Tenchita,
hoy quiero decirte
that your feelings of abandonment
when *papá* came to the U.S.
to take you back to México
with *mamá* and your sisters
those feelings are valid.

Sí, *tu papá no tuvo los pantalones*
para llevarte de regreso a México.
Sí, Tenchita,
me duele decirte que tu papá
te abandonó,
te falló.

And in this painful truth,
we can also hold space
for his grief,
for the sorrow he carried
when he left you behind.

You were too small to understand,
but I am here now
the adult you
to tell you:
Tu papá te amaba profundamente
Y sufrió en silencio tu ausencia.

His love for you
was so deep
that he made an impossible choice
to leave you behind,
so you could have a better future,
a better education,
para ti, para la familia
Y futuras generaciones

Section 2
Roots and Memory: La Tierra en Mis Huesos

Nopalera con Orgullo

Soy nopalera,
nopalera con orgullo.

Nopalera,
you know how to survive
and thrive
in the harshest conditions
sun-scorched,
wind-blown,
still blooming.

Soft and tender por dentro,
tus espinas are not weakness
they are your armor
against injustice,
oppression,
and every force that's tried
to erase you.

You are amor tierno
and amor feroz,
a love that protects,
a love that resists.

Nopalera,
stand tall in your culture,
in your identity
porque you are living proof
of your ancestors' strength.

May you continue to thrive
when life gets dry,
when the soil cracks,
when loneliness creeps in.

Remember
you are never alone.

Tienes comunidad.
Tienes otros nopalitos
rooting for you,
growing beside you,
watching you bloom
con cada rayo de sol.

Nopalera,
you are paving the way
for future generations
little nopalitos
who will learn to love their thorns
because of you.

Protect your heart,
your joy,
your sacred energy
with these beautiful thorns,
con estas espinas
que son escudo,
not a weapon
Espinas that guard
but never wound.

Nopalera,
sigue floreciendo
con orgullo

Borders

Imaginary borders,
physical borders,
emotional borders,
spiritual borders,
cultural borders,
we all know borders in one form or another.

The U.S.–Mexico border,
a wound too familiar
for those of us who are of Mexican descent
Central American
Latin American
anyone who has walked the long road
from home to el otro lado.

Crossing la frontera
is more than a physical act
it's emotional,
it's spiritual.

It's the ache of leaving
what we once called home,
and la familia we never stopped loving.
Some of us didn't choose to come.

We were brought here
by displacement,
by necessity,
by economic, political, and social circumstances.

Some crossed deserts with empty stomachs
and trembling hands,
risking life for survival,
for hope,
for a chance.

Cruzando la frontera te marca para siempre
It leaves a mark that never fades
You carry the recuerdos,
the sazón y olor de las comidas,
the lullabies and tradiciones
that no border wall can erase.

We bring with us
rich culture,
ancestral wisdom
proof that spirit travels freely,
cuts through borders like light.

But the pain is real
The separation,
the silence of years gone by,
decades without tus seres queridos

Even when reunion comes,
it's never the same.
Time doesn't return;
you ask yourself ¿valió la pena?

Was it worth the papers,
the education,
the promise to one day help your family?
The price is heavy.
The grief is immense.

Grief for the homeland,
for the birthdays missed,
for the family celebrations,
for not saying goodbye to your loved ones.

I grieve the niña inside me
who was separated from her parents and sisters
I grieve still,
as a grown woman
without shame,
without denial of the pain.

Because this is the truth of borders

they divide,
they wound.

They fragment family ties
and still,
we find ways
to love across them.

Mixed Status Families

I come from a mixed-status family
I crossed into this country sin papeles,
a niña carrying the weight of hope sin saber.
Through the amnistía of the 1980s
I was granted the so called green card.

At twenty-one I became a naturalized citizen,
so I could open the opportunity
for my family left behind.
In 2001 I filed the papers,
in 2003 my mother received her green card.

My sisters are still waiting
waiting for their numbers,
waiting for a call,
waiting to reunite
with my undocumented sister
they haven't seen
in over twenty-five years.

The grief I carry is valid.
So is my privilege
A citizen's passport
doesn't erase
a sister's tears.

Being from a mixed-status family
is an ache en el corazón
Even now, under a government
that sharpens laws
against our brown existence,
we live in hypervigilance
hearts racing with anxiety,
bodies remembering separation,
our spirit learning to regulate its nervous system.
while never fully safe

Papers don't protect us
from the trauma of
family separation,
deportations,
the fear of a knock at the car or house door,
the silence after goodbye.

Inside our homes,
resentments simmer:
¿Por qué tú sí y yo no?
Why do you have papers
and I don't?
Why are you a citizen
and I'm still lost in the system's maze?

Being part of a mixed-status family
is an emotional roller coaster
love tangled with grief,
privilege tangled with guilt,
belonging tangled with exile.

To all my mixed-status families:
I see you.
I honor you.
Your grief is sacred,
your resilience unbreakable
Our stories are messy,
complex,
and beautifully human.
We are the living proof
that borders cannot divide
Love.

Comida de Rancho

Nopales recién cortados
beans simmering in the pot,
freshly made tortillas, water from the well.
Verdolagas, champiñones,
corn ground and pressed into life,
a metate weaving tradition into every bite.

Fresh salsa from the molcajete,
queso fresco, panela, jocoqui,
corn freshly harvested, roasted, dried
so it carries us through the rainy season.

Estas comidas de rancho,
por más simples, son riquísimas.
Una conexión con los animales y la Madre Tierra

Never be ashamed of your cultural foods.
They are memory, preservation, resistance,
part of who we are, part of our survival.

Because our cultural foods are more than food
son memoria,
son historia,
they are resistance,
they are part of our existence.

Salinas

Salinas,
located in Monterey County,
known across the world
as the "Salad Bowl" of the World
though most don't know her that way.

They know Pebble Beach,
its coastal wealth,
the Concours d'Elegance,
Carmel-by-the-Sea, Big Sur, Pacific Grove
postcards of beautiful beaches.

But to get to their beauty,
you passed us.
Highway 68 or Highway 1,
you blinked,
and missed an entire city
of people full of corazón.

Salinas may not shimmer
with coastal mansions,
but she is rich.
Rich in culture,
in traditions,
in families that know how to survive,
and still offer you a plate of food.

Here, our cultural murals bloom on walls
like prayers,
like memory,
like resistance.
Here, immigrant and farmworker families
carry the weight of feeding the nation.

Salinas has been given names,
Gang City, Violent City, Less Educated City.
But beneath every label,
lives a deeper story.
A town where families struggle
below the poverty line,
where *la comunidad* hustles
one, two, sometimes three jobs
just to stay afloat.

Where single mothers,
true superheroes
carry their children,
hold the home together,
and still keep the local economy alive.

Where youth search
for spaces to breathe, to be,
to dream,
to simply exist.

Still yet,
Salinas grows brilliance.
First generation students,
first in their families,
first to dare
to break a path where none existed.

Some leave,
and the ache of their leaving
is felt in their families heart and in our comunidad.

Some return,
educators, nurses, doctors, lawyers, healers, artists,
advocates, entrepreneurs
coming home to lift what lifted them.

Salinas,
land of the Salinan,
Ohlone, Rumsen, Mutsun
still present and fighting for their recognition.

We are Salinas.
We are here.
We are rooted.
We are a reflection of what is possible.

I honor you, Salinas.

I love you, Salinas.
Even when dreaming big is heavy,
even when being first means being alone,
we continue to break barriers.

We continue to break barriers
for ourselves,
for our families,
for the generations to come.

Because this city
this beautiful and hardworking city,
has always been more than the world chose to see.

Soy de Rancho

Soy de rancho,
vengo de la Madre Sierra Occidental,
del estado de Nayarit,
del gran Nayar.

Soy de rancho,
orgullosa de ser ranchera,
orgullosa de ser del Pinal, Municipio de la Yesca.
Lo que antes fue vergüenza,
un insulto en la boca de la gente,
hoy lo abrazo con orgullo,
con la frente en alto.

Tener raíces de rancho no es vergüenza,
al contrario, es orgullo.
Orgullo de vivir de lo que provee la Madre Tierra,
de estar en relación con ella,
de escuchar su pulso en la vida diaria.

Ser de rancho es uno de mis orgullos más grandes.
Es quien soy,
es mi conexión con mis ancestros.

Las vacas, los caballos, las gallinas, el burro, los perros...
la vida de rancho es hermosa.
Pero también es dolorosa
pobreza profunda,
educación ausente,
niñas casándose antes de cumplir los dieciocho.

La vida de rancho es hermosa,
pero llena de sueños que chocan
con la falta de oportunidades.
Donde apenas había unos cuantos carros,
electricidad escasa,
una escuelita,
y una casita de adobe que servía de iglesia,
donde el padre llegaba a misa en burro,
en caballo,
y a veces, con suerte, en carro.

La vida de rancho es hermosa,
pero triste.
Un rancho con una sola tiendita.
Con un solo conasupo con precios exagerados,
un mundo donde las mujeres eran vistas
solo para casarse,
tener hijos,
cocinar, lavar, cuidar de la cosecha
y servir a su esposo.

La vida de rancho es hermosa,
pero limita a las niñas,
a las mujeres.
Mi padre dejó la sierra con mi madre y mis
hermanas,
todo en una camioneta
sueños, recuerdos,
y pocas pertenencias.
Del rancho a Guadalajara,
una travesía por un futuro mejor.

Un futuro que aún duele,
cuando los padres solo tenían
tercer grado de educación,
pero una vida llena de sabiduría
sabían de la tierra,
de los animales,
pero no de la gran ciudad.

La vida de rancho es hermosa,
pero no hay que romantizarla.
Hay pobreza.
Hay hambre.
Hay violencia.
Hay ausencia de oportunidades.

Quienes logramos salir,
cruzar al otro lado,
como yo,
pagamos un precio doloroso
la separación,
la distancia de mis padres y hermanas,
para poder tener una educación
Un futuro mejor.

La vida de rancho es hermosa,
pero deja cicatrices.
Deja heridas y duelos por la tierra madre,
porque nunca podré volver a vivir ahí,
ya no es seguro.

La vida de rancho es hermosa
Pero deja nostalgia del gran Nayar,
Del Pinal, de la Sierra Madre Occidental.
Pero llevo el rancho en mi piel y en mi corazón,
para siempre.

Estoy orgullosa de mis raíces,
llevo el nopal en la frente
con orgullo de ser de rancho.

El Amor de Mi Madre No Conoce Fronteras

Madrecita linda y hermosa,
sé que sufrió por mi ausencia.
No puedo imaginar
el dolor,
la tristeza,
la soledad,
el duelo
de no tener a una de tus hijas
a su lado.

Así como usted me extraño,
yo también la extrañé profundamente.
De niña no entendía
por qué estaba tan lejos
de mis hermanas,
de mis padres,
de tus brazos
de su amor afectuoso.

Por cosas del destino
la frontera nos separó,
pero nunca pudo separar
nuestro amor
ni nuestro corazón.

El tiempo no regresa,
lo sé.
Solo tenemos el presente,

Me siento profundamente orgullosa
de tener una madre tan fuerte como usted.
Usted me enseño
el amor incondicional
un amor que existe
más allá de cualquier frontera.

Gracias por tus enseñanzas,
por sus consejos,
por sus sabiduría,
por sus remedios.
Pero, sobre todo,
gracias por su amor.

Soy una mujer fuerte
porque vengo
de una madre fuerte y valiente
como usted.

Gracias por darme la vida Madrecita linda!

Home

Home is not about place,
it's about feeling safe.

It's the warm *cariño*
de tus amistades,
a lick from your dog,
a smile when you see
una *chuparrosa.*

Our ancestors
did not attach home
to a place,
or a building,
or a structure.

Home is where you are held,
not walls that confine you.

Western society
and colonialism
have made us believe
that home
is a structure
with four walls.

But instead of those walls
why not fall in love
with the idea
that the four elements
are home?

Earth.
Air.
Fire.
Water.

You will always find home
within yourself
not in people,
not in places,
not in geography.

Home is returning,
living,
and residing
within you.

You are home
and you will always be home,
no matter how many times
you move,
are relocated,
displaced,
or abandoned.

Come home
to yourself.

My Brown Skin

My brown skin holds stories,
memorias tristes y dulces.

But my brown skin
also carries my ancestors'
medicine,
wisdom,
songs,
rhythm,
sunlight,
resiliency woven in my trenzas,
and queer love that refuses to be erased.

I wear my brown skin
with pride,
with joy,
with every breath
that says:
I love my brown skin!
Amo mi piel morena!

Academia

Academia stripped me of my voice.
Taught me to speak in tongues
that never belonged to me.
Academic jargon polished enough
to make it into peer-reviewed journals,
yet unreadable to my community,
incomprehensible to my family.

As a doctoral student,
I sat in conference rooms
listening to colleagues speak
in languages of theory and abstraction,
and still, I felt stupid,
out of place,
like I had no right to be there,

But that is academia.
The elitism,
the need to sound intelligent
to be seen as worthy.
As if brilliance lives only
in vocabulary and theory.

As if my family
with their calloused hands,
their wrinkled face,
their white hair,
telling decades of testiomino y sabiduria
that no academic journal will ever publish.

Their wisdom shaped by survival
were anything less than smart.

Academia tried to take my voice,
but I have been gathering it back
piece by piece.
Learning to hear myself again
beyond the ivory tower,
beyond the conditioning,
beyond the fear.

I am reclaiming the voice
they told me to quiet.
I am returning to the one
I was born with.
The one rooted in comunidad,
in truth, in me.

Unapologetic Spanglish

Soy una Mexicana inmigrante,
con orgullo profundo de mis raíces.
I am proud of being a Mexican immigrant,
of speaking both Spanish and English.

De gozar mis comidas culturales
mis tamalitos, tortillas, pozole, enchiladas,
frijoles recién hechos de la olla
and I also enjoy American food
apple pie, pizza,
y sí, hamburgers too.

Being bicultural is beautiful,
yet you are never fully one thing.

Nunca eres "lo suficiente Mexicana,"
aunque naciste en México,
creciste en México,
visitaste México,
o tienes familia en México.

Nunca eres "lo suficiente Mexicana"
cuando cruzas al otro lado,
al Norte.
Y ya en el Norte,
nuestra gente en México nos ve como Americanos,
but we will never be American.

Yes, North American by continent,
but never fully American in U.S soil
Our skin color,
our accent,
our ancestry,
our cultural foods
remind us of the borders
we carry inside
and enforced by others.

A veces bicultural
nunca fully accepted
ni allá ni aqui.
So I embrace my Spanglish.
Aunque para algunos sea ofensa
"no hablas buen español,"
"you're butchering el idioma,"
nos da vergüenza.

Pero Spanglish is essence.
It is disruption.
It is refusal of binaries.
It is embracing both tongues,
en nuestros propios términos.

There is power in how we speak.

I embrace Spanglish
because it is who I am.

Fluent in Spanish,
fluent in English,
fluent en Spanglish
that too is fluency.

Many first, second, and third generation,
pierden el español completo,
y Spanglish se vuelve lengua dominante.
And that is ok.

Never apologize for your Spanglish.
It is who you are.
It is your experience.

Being Spanglish is not easy
weaving two languages
is skill,
is art,
is survival.

Lazy? Nunca.
Skillful, yes.
A mirror of our identities.
Spanglish es resistencia.
Spanglish es memoria.
Spanglish es amor.

Spanglish es mi lengua.

Soy Hija de la Madre Tierra

Soy hija de la Madre Tierra,
sus raíces corren por mis venas,
me sostienen, me anclan,
son mi fortaleza.

Escucho el pálpito de su corazón,
tun tun de amor puro,
amor incondicional
que me recuerda
el regalo de la vida,
la vida que tengo,
la vida que tenemos.

Todo lo que necesito
ella me lo provee.

Soy hija de la Madre Tierra
su suelo fértil, su lodo,
parte de mi ser.
Cuando muera, ceniza seré,
y en su suelo fértil volveré.

Soy hija de la Madre Tierra
ella me alumbra y me guía
con su luz en la oscuridad.
En las tormentas,
en los momentos difíciles,
me recuerda que la claridad
habita en mí,
que tengo mi propia luz interior
para guiar mi andar.

Soy hija de la Madre Tierra
llena de vida,
de amor, de fuego.
Ese fuego a veces titila
como mechita pequeña,
pero también arde grande,
amplio y fuerte,
capaz de iluminar
el camino de otros.

Soy hija de la Madre Tierra

su aire me abraza,
me levanta en lo difícil,
me acompaña en la salud,
en la risa, en la alegría y las tristezas

Soy hija de la Madre Tierra.
Siempre me arropa,
siempre me sostiene.

Still Blooming

She's not just strong in the gym.
She's strong for surviving a society that told her to
shrink and stay calladita.
She's healing intergenerational wounds.
She's eating her tamales, tortillas, frijoles y
nopalitos,
and speaking her truth.
She's reclaiming joy without apology.
She is me.
I'm not done growing, evolving, or blooming.

Frijolera con Orgullo

Frijolera,
soy frijolera con orgullo.

I love beans.
They are my connection
to culture,
to identidad,
to my ancestors.

What others once called
"comida de pobre,"
"poor people's food,"
"sin clase"...
is actually
sacred,
sustaining,
ancestral abundance
that fed my family
in times of hunger,
and shortages.

Frijolera con orgullo
porque los frijoles
son pura cultura.

Don't let anyone treat you
like frijoles de lata
cuando eres frijoles de la olla,
slow-cooked
con sazón,
con amor,
y pura cultura.

You are not microwave energy.
You are made-from-scratch energy.
You ARE ancestral recipe energy.

Sabor so rich,
it doesn't need validation.
Some will try to box you in,
make you shrink,
make you settle.
¡Pero NO!

You're flavor-full,
soul-fed,
heart-healing.

Frijolera,
never forget
you are tradition,
you are resistance,
you are orgullo!

Vengo de un Linaje de Mujeres Fuertes

Vengo de un linaje de mujeres fuertes,
mujeres sabias,
mujeres luchonas,
mujeres medicina.

Vengo de un linaje de curanderas,
de mujeres de fe,
donde el catolicismo y las prácticas indígenas
coexistían,
no uno o el otro,
sino ambos entrelazados
como una trenza

Vengo de un linaje de mujeres trabajadoras,
inteligentes y sabias,
aunque nunca les dieron la oportunidad
de recibir educación formal.
No tuvieron elección.
Se casaron jóvenes
o fueron robadas por el novio,
y ahí terminaron sus sueños.

Pero aun sin escuela,
llevaban consigo la sabiduría ancestral,
la medicina heredada,
pasada de generación en generación
como un fuego que nunca se apaga.

Vengo de un linaje de mujeres fuertes
que tuvieron que ocultar su sexualidad.
Las mujeres de mi linajes
no podían ser queer,
no podían amar en libertad.

Hasta ahora
Yo rompo esa cadena,
No guardo mas secretos
No guardo más vergüenza

I release this shame
I release any secrets
I break this intergenerational chain of oppression

Yo abro este nuevo camino
Soy la primera en abrazar mi queerness
abiertamente, con orgullo.

Lo hago por mí,
pero también por ellas,
las que nunca pudieron serlo.

Porque todas las mujeres en mi linaje
viven en mí.
Yo soy ellas,
y ellas son yo.

Allow Mother Earth

Allow Mother Earth
to wrap you in her wind,
to ground you with her soil,
to cleanse and purify you with her waters,
to ignite your heart with her fire.
So you may feel deeply,
and never lose
your humanity,
and your light.

Trenzas

Every night,
I braid my hair.
Not out of habit,
but out of memory.

Before my hands learned the rhythm,
my abuelita braided for me,
her fingers steady,
patient, ancestral.
She braided care into my scalp,
love into each crossing strand con un liston,
until I was old enough
to carry the ritual on my own.

My long hair is not vanity
It is homage
An offering to the women before me
who were told to cut,
to tame,
to erase,
to conform.

My long hair is resistance,
a refusal of colonial scissors,
a quiet rebellion against forgetting.

Each trenza says:
I am still here.
¡Aquí sigo!
Braiding my hair is my prayer.

Each pull,
a grounding.
Each twist,
a conversation with my ancestors.
I braid in silence,
and they answer in warmth,
in memory,
in strength,
In wisdom.

Mis trenzas son parte de mi identidad
of my many, layered, intersecting selves.
Just like a braid,
I am made of many threads.
I do not separate who I am
to make others comfortable.

My trenzas refuse compartments.
They remind me
that I can be all of me
at once.

Mis trenzas are rebellion.
Mis trenzas are lineage.
They carry the stories, the grief, the joy,
the survival of those who came before.

I carry my ancestors on my head,
with pride.
They are my superpower,
my grounding,
my resilience.

I am rooted in my braids,
anchored in my long hair.
Because I do not walk alone,
I carry my ancestors with me.

Not Neutral

Complacency
is not neutral.

Neutrality
in the face of injustice
is a choice
and it sides with harm.

Tus ancestros
no cruzaron desiertos, ríos, fronteras
no sobrevivieron guerras,
no aguantaron violencia y silencios
para que tú
te quedaras mirando
desde la orilla.

They did not fight
for their existence
so you could be a bystander.

Ellos lucharon
con cuerpo,
con espíritu,
con amor feroz.

You must fight

for justice,
for what is right,
for what is sacred

Le debes a tus ancestros
and to the ones
who will come after you
to create a world less cruel,
more compassionate,
more tolerant, and
more loving.

Stand up.
Speak up.
Resist.

This is your inheritance.
This is your offering.
This is your legacy.

ICE

ICE arrives without warning.
Not the kind that falls softly from the sky,
but the kind that is hard, deliberate,
meant to bruise, meant to harm,
meant to cause pain.

ICE arrives.
Sin aviso.
No weather forecast.
Just cold intent
wrapped in uniforms,
faces covered.

ICE separates by design.
Ese es el propósito.
Freezes mothers on one side of the glass,
fathers on the other,
children suspended in the cold.

¿Dónde está mi mamá?
¿Dónde está mi papá?
¿Cuándo regresan?

ICE does not just deport people.
It deports sleep.
El sueño.
It deports safety.
It deports dreams and aspirations.
It deports the nervous system.
La seguridad de caminar sin miedo.

La gente habla.
ICE sprays them.
La gente protesta.
ICE golpea, empuja.

People speak,
and ICE punishes them for it.
People march,
and ICE bruises their right to exist loudly.

Amendments melt in its presence.
People of color become a target temperature.
Accents become probable cause.
Fear becomes a daily climate.

We learn to live layered.
We learn to live con miedo.
We learn to live con frio.
Mirando por encima del hombro.
Guardando papeles como rosarios.

Documents clutched
like life depends on it
because it does.
Teaching children what to do
si *no regresan sus padres...*
But ICE forgets something.

ICE is not permanent.
ICE is temporary.
ICE is fragile.
ICE cannot survive fire.
ICE melts con calor.
Con fuego.
Con coraje.
Con amor organizado.

ICE cannot withstand collective breath,
cannot hold shape
when comunidad shows up.

ICE melts when rage becomes organized.
When grief becomes movement.
When love refuses to be frozen.

The only way I like ICE
is crushed.
Hecho pedacitos.
Incapaz de separar.
Incapaz de aterrorizar.
Porque este hielo no es natural.

Este frío no es natural.
Y ningún sistema de hielo
sobrevive
a un pueblo
que sabe cómo hacer fuego
con comunidad,
con memoria,
con amor que no se deja congelar.

The only way I like ICE
is shattered.
Crushed.
Reduced to something powerless,
at the bottom of a glass,
sweating, disappearing,
no longer able to harm.

Liberating the Ancestors

Erotic embodiment...
is divine life force.
Because it connects...
to Mother Earth,
to the ancestors
who couldn't embrace
their erotic energy.

To the ancestors
who suppressed
their pleasure.

You...
You are liberating the ancestors
every time you embody
your erotic energy.

As resistance.
As healing.
As radical self-love.

You are divine.
You are whole.
You have arrived.
You are alive.
You are enough.

Your body...
exactly as it is
is worthy.

Worthy of tenderness,
of touch,
of love,
of pleasure.

Worthy...
of fully feeling
the erotic energy
flowing through you

Erotic embodiment
is divine life force
Es el corazón palpitando,
reminding you
You are alive.

Section 3
Me Elijo: Reclaiming Self, Voice, and Autonomy

I Hate the Patriarchy and I Love Men

I hate the patriarchy and I love men,
this is not a contradiction
but the reality that men are not inherently
patriarchal,
sexist, misogynist, or machistas.

Men, especially the men in our lives,
en nuestra cultura no nacieron machistas, se
hicieron.
They were socialized and conditioned
to internalize and uphold patriarchal values
that men are superior to women,
that a woman's role is to embrace
traditional feminine roles,
to be the caretakers and nurturers del hogar.

Amo a los hombres
and I hate the patriarchy
that has harmed men with toxic masculinity,
that tough guise,
esa máscara que dice
que los hombres no lloran,
que los hombres no son mandilones,
que llevan los pantalones en la casa.

I hate the patriarchy that teaches men
to oppress women,
to see them as sexual objects for their pleasure,
to value them for their physical appearance,
to label them as damaged goods
if they lose their virginity,
if they are sexually assaulted,
if they are getting too old,
too wrinkled,
too human.

I hate the patriarchy that oppresses women
and harms men.

I hate the patriarchy
and I love men who have the courage
to work on their healing,
the men who decide to end
the intergenerational violence,
the trauma,
the toxic masculinity,
and heteronormative values.

I love men who are so confident
and secure in themselves
that they are not embarrassed or ashamed
to express their feelings,
who cry,
who communicate with love and compassion,
who hold space for their women,
nosotras las guerreras.

I hate the patriarchy
and I love men who honor women
in their multidimensionality,
in their complexity,
in their messiness,
in their humanity.

Men who are not scared
of strong-minded, independent women,
who are go-getters,
trailblazers,
the first in their family to earn an education,
a profession,
who are entrepreneurs, lawyers, doctors
the first in everything.

I hate the patriarchy
and I love men who uplift their women
and all the women around them.

I love men who are able to acknowledge
their male and heterosexual privilege
and use it to be upstanders,
to be allies,
who know when to remain silent
so that women can speak,
who don't take up space unnecessarily.

I love men who say,
"I see too many men in this space,
we need more female representation."
Men who take a step back,
who decline opportunities
when there is an overrepresentation of men
and a lack of women.
Men who give up their seat
so another woman can be represented.

Let's be clear
this is not men doing us a favor,
this is not the patriarchy.
This is men who have done their healing,
who are divesting from patriarchal structures
that continue to oppress women.

I hate the patriarchy
and I love men
who are not intimidated
by strong, outspoken, brilliant,
and just plain badass women
who have bad bitch energy.

This, to me,
is hot and sexy.

I Move to the Beat of My Own Drum

I move to the beat of my own drum,
to the rhythm of *mi corazón,*
ese corazón que late con amor,
with truth, with rhythm,
with divine intention.

I move to the beat of divine timing
what's meant for me
will arrive when it's ready.
I just have to trust the process,
trust myself,
trust Spirit,
God,
and my ancestors
that they are guiding me,
holding me.

I move to the beat of my intuition
in a world that's forgotten
its own heartbeat,
a world disconnected from Spirit,
from *el corazón,*
from intuition,
from ancestral knowing.

I move to the beat of trust,
feeling it deep in my bones
what's meant for me
will come
when it's meant to.

You can label me,
you can judge me,
call me *loca* if you must,
that's okay.
You don't have to understand
what I feel
so deeply
in *mi corazón,*
en mi piel,
en mi cuerpo.

Because I carry
my ancestors' strength,
their wisdom,
their DNA,
I trust that I am never alone,
never abandoned.

My ancestors and Creator
walk beside me,
especially in the dark
when pain feels endless,
when life feels heavy.
That's when they carry me,
move with me,
at my own rhythm,
my own heartbeat,
but never alone.

Deep in your bones
is where you'll find
the strength,
the resilience
to keep moving forward
at *your* pace,
not the world.

Show Up for Yourself

How do you expect to show up for others
if you forget to show up for yourself?

The way I show up for me
may not be the way others show up for me
and that's ok.
I must remain loyal to myself,
integral to myself,
home to myself.

I won't lie
it hurts
when others don't show up
the way you deserve,
the way you show up for them.
But don't lose yourself
trying to hold on.
Don't gaslight your own heart
into believing
you deserve mistreatment or disrespect.

You are too good for that shit.

Loyalty to yourself
is the most radical act of love.
Honor yourself first,
because if you don't
no one else will.

You must model
what it means to show up for yourself,
so others know how to meet you there.

You are not asking too much.
You are not too much.
What you ask for
is the most basic
love, respect, reciprocity.

Yet many don't have the capacity.
But you do.

So keep showing up for yourself.
Keep being authentic to your truth.
Keep being unapologetically you.
Keep being
the most beautiful human
in this world.

Dreams Do Not Have an Expiration

Dreams do not have an expiration date.

Silence the voices,
tune up your inner knowing,
your trust in the Creator
and surrender.

Surrender,
and keep working toward your goals,
because with your every day actions
you will get closer to your dreams.

Dreams do not have an expiration date.

We have been gaslighted
to believe we must accomplish certain goals
at a certain age,
at a certain point in our lives.
Fuck that!
That is rooted in systems of oppression,
capitalism,
and values of productivity and professionalism.

Dreams do not have an expiration date
because you are unique,
on your own unique and beautiful journey.

Believe that where you are
is where you're meant to be.
The goals and dreams that you hold
will come in divine timing.

Tap into your ancestral wisdom.
Tap into your inner knowing.
Tap into trust and surrender.

Surrender to the process.
Surrendering does not mean giving up
it means trusting divine timing,
trusting the Creator,
trusting your ancestors
and all your guardian angels
who are guiding you in this life.

Hold tight to your goals,
your aspirations,
your dreams
and surrender.

Keep working toward your goals,
no matter the obstacles,
no matter how many no's,
rejections,
or people who say
you're dreaming too high,
that it's impossible,
that you shouldn't dare
to imagine that goal.

We have been conditioned
for immediate gratification,
and I'm here to tell you
that is part of the problem.

Embrace delayed gratification.
Trust.
Surrender.

Because your dreams
do not have an expiration date.

Dreams do not have an expiration date.

Don't compare your journey to others
that is a setup
for failure,
for feeling inadequate.

It is a disservice
to your own journey,
your lived experience,
your intersecting identities.

Some dreams take longer to bloom
and that is okay.

Your dreams
do not have
an expiration date.

Reclamation

I am reclaiming every single part of me.
Every part that has been denied,
Every part I was forced to hide,
Every part that was shamed into silence.

I am reclaiming my voice.
My senses,
My erotic energy,
My intellect and my opinions.
I am reclaiming my wholeness,
something I've struggled with all my life.

Reclaiming wholeness means taking back even the
parts I was taught to hate,
the parts I was conditioned to exile.
It means opening the door to the hidden,
and saying *you belong, too.*

Reclaiming every single part of me
is a radical act of self-love.

Reclamation is on my own terms.
Not at the cost of my authenticity.

Not at the cost of my values.

Not at the cost of my integrity.

When you reclaim your wholeness,
when you gather the pieces others tried to break
apart and dim,
the pieces shamed into shadows,
you ignite something sacred and powerful.
Reclamation becomes both love and resistance.

But reclamation is not easy.
Because others will hold on to the old versions of
you.
They will try to keep you one-dimensional,
digestible.

Still...
I reclaim myself anyway.
Every wound, every joy,
every contradiction, every messiness, every truth.

Because wholeness is not perfection.
Wholeness, not permission.
Wholeness is power.
Wholeness is freedom.

Wholeness is love for myself.

Wholeness is sovereignty.

Wholeness is coming to myself.

I am whole.

Me Elijo

Me elijo todos los días
Aunque me tiemble la voz,
Aunque llore cuando hable mi verdad
Aunque el mundo me diga
Que me calle,
to stop being too opinionated,
too critical,
too passionate,
too sensitive.

I choose myself
again and again,
without apology.

I will not abandon myself
for anything
or anyone
that is not in alignment
with my spirit,
mi corazón, y
mi camino.

Me elijo.
Hoy.
Mañana.
Siempre.

Choosing Yourself

Choosing yourself, radically,
means embracing pain,
embracing fear,
embracing rejection.

No one tells you
that choosing yourself every fucking day
means letting go of people
who've been in your life for years,
maybe even decades.

Choosing yourself radically
means honoring boundaries,
honoring your integrity,
honoring your values.

It means shedding societal standards
how you "should" be,
how you "should" behave,
how you "should" conform.

Choosing yourself radically
is not for the weak.
It is walking through uncharted waters,
terrains unknown,
terrains that terrify,
terrains you may cross alone.

It means sitting in solitude,
being with yourself,
by yourself,
embracing all of you fully.

It means releasing the old version of you,
letting go of limiting narratives,
transmuting pain into healing.

Choosing yourself radically
means refusing bullshit,
setting high standards,
leading with integrity.

It means you may stand alone.
Others won't understand
and it's not your job to make them.
It's your job to embrace yourself.

Choosing yourself radically
means never betraying yourself,
never allowing mistreatment,
never allowing shame to define you.

It means honoring every version of you
past, present, and future you.

Yes, it's hard work.
But you must believe in yourself.

Choosing yourself radically
is the best gift you can give yourself.
Not everyone has the courage.
It's painful,
but within the pain
there is light,
there is hope,
there is joy
there is freedom.

Because choosing yourself radically
is loving yourself,
knowing you don't *need* anyone.
Whoever enters your life
adds to it
a choice, not a necessity.

This goes for friends,
for intimate relationships,
for every kind of relationship.

Choose yourself radically,
every day.
Some days you'll cruise,
some days you'll stumble on rocks.

It is a rollercoaster,
non-linear,
messy, raw, alive.

And still
the most sacred,
the most powerful,
the most beautiful gift
you can give yourself
every day
is choosing and loving yourself.

I Won't Betray Myself

I won't betray myself
Repeat after me
I WON'T BETRAY MYSELF!
I choose myself radically
EVERYDAY!

I Reclaim My Own Autonomy

I reclaim my own autonomy
In my own terms,
No lo que dice la sociedad,
La familia,
Las amistades,
No!
I reclaim my own autonomy
As it aligns with my values.
My authenticity.
No me importa
Si no te parece.

Creo en Mi

Creo en mi
Aun cuando los demás dudan y juzgan

Creo en mi potencial
De alcanzar las estrellas
Sin importar que tan lejos están

Creo en mi vulnerabilidad
Y lagrimas
como signo de fortaleza

Creo en mi cuando
Lloro
Cuando estoy nerviosa
Cuando me tiemblan las manos
When my voice cracks

Creo en mi even
When no one else en la familia has done
What I dare to dream

Creo en mi aún
When there is no clear path ahead
But a deep inner knowing
Que mis ancestros me guian

Creo en mi porque
Mis ancestros viven en mi
Me guian,
They whisper
"You got this mija"
No olvides que vienes de un linaje
De mujeres fuertes y sabias

Creo en mi!

Me Prometo

Me prometo amarme
y aceptarme tal y como soy.
I promise myself
not to betray myself for anyone.

Me prometo estar ahí para mí,
I promise myself
to show up for myself
every day,
en días felices,
on happy days,
en días nublados,
on gloomy days,
en días tristes,
on sad days,
en días depresivos,
on depressive days,
en días de alegría,
on joyful days,
en días emocionantes,
on exciting days,
en días difíciles.
on difficult days.

Me prometo levantarme por mí
cada día,
en cada versión de mí.
I promise myself
to show up for myself
every day
in every iteration of myself.

In every messy version of myself
No tiene que ser perfecto.
It doesn't have to be perfect.
Esa no es la meta.
That's not the goal.
The goal is to show up for myself
Because doing so is also for everyone else
La meta is to show up for me
cada día,
exactamente como soy.
The goal is to show up for myself
every day,
exactly as I am
por mí,
para mí,
no para nadie más.
For myself,
not for anyone else.

El Cambio es Incómodo Pero...

El cambio es incómodo pero necesario.
Change is uncomfortable but necessary.
We are conditioned and socialized
to hold on
to material things,
to a house,
to a partner,
to people,
to work,
to friendships.

Pero a veces,
change is necessary,
and yes,
it's uncomfortable.
It's painful.
It's scary.

El cambio es incómodo
porque requiere crecimiento,
it requires trust in yourself,
silencing external voices,
quieting the voices you've internalized
about who you are,
how you should act,
what you should believe,
do,
and be.

Change is uncomfortable
because it challenges
everything you've been conditioned
to believe, to do.
Es incómodo porque
no le vas a caer bien a todos.
People will not always agree
with your choices,
with your lifestyle.

El cambio es incómodo pero necesario
si queremos crecer,
evolucionar,
shed,
release,
transmute,
keep growing.

El cambio es incómodo pero necesario
y también puede ser hermoso y liberador
lleno de oportunidades.

Opportunities are waiting for you,
pero tienes que dar
ese primer paso.

Believe in yourself.
Trust en el cambio
Porque
El cambio es incómodo pero necesario.

Trust

Trust the process.
Trust your intuition.
Trust your divine timing.
Trust and surrender.
El universo nunca se equivoca.

Divine Timing

Time
Timelines
Urgency culture
where worth is measured
in how much,
how fast,
how perfectly we produce.

Productivity,
professionalism,
socialization
all say the same lie: *you're behind.*

"No crezcas, cuál es la prisa,"
they say when we're young.
Then suddenly *you should be grown by now.*
"What are you going to do?"
"¿Y el novio?"
"¿Cuándo te vas a casar?"
"¿Y los hijos?"

We live in contradictions.
They don't want us to grow up too fast,
but then demand we have it all figured out
by the time we're barely learning
who we are.

This pressure,
this *urgency*
is a wound disguised as love.

You are not late.
You are not early.
You are in your own divine timing.

Time is a social construct, sí,
but before colonial clocks
and calendars carved our days,
our ancestors
moved with the rhythm of the seasons,
listened to the sun,
to the rain,
to the body,
to the earth.
May you return to that rhythm,
to the sacred slowness
of being.
Hortencia

Hortencia

That's my name.
Not HORtencia,
it's Hortencia.
I am tired of constantly telling and correcting folks
that H is silent in Spanish
and you pronounce the O,
Hortencia.

My name has been butchered
all my life,
desde niña chiquita
Cómo lo odiaba,
How I hated
and was ashamed of my name.

In truth
I still haven't fully embraced my name
It carries so much pain,
so much mispronunciation,
so many kids made fun of my name growing up.

Kids in elementary school can be cruel
and that pain still lingers
in my inner niña.
I'm still on the journey
de amar y abrazar mi nombre

In truth,
I don't know if I will ever love my name
but right now I can tell you
that I accept it
I honor it
I am proud of it
I honor my name
I am proud of my name
yet I do not love it.

I do not need to love my name
to accept it.
My name does not have a deep meaning
When I asked my mamá
she told me she named me Hortencia
because she heard it from a neighbor
and she thought it was a nice name.

As a teenager I found out
that my name is actually
the name of a Mexican flower,
and I really never bothered to look up the flower
because I hated my name.

Truth be told
I looked up the flower about 6 years ago
and wow...
What a beautiful flower.

Hortensia in English is Hydrangea,
a beautiful, large and colorful flower cluster.
"Hortensia" is an old-fashioned common name
for some varieties of hydrangea.

Hydrangea
large clusters,
blue, pink, purple, or white,
depending on soil,
and requiring a lot of water.

The meaning of hydrangea comes from Greek
words
for "water" and "vessel,"
referring to its high water needs.
I can say that it would have been nice
to have a name with Indigenous origins,
but that's the name my mom named me
and I honor it.

The more I come to embrace Hortencia,
hydrangea flower,
the more I realize I have in common.
Water vessel,
one of the sacred elements.
We are water.
And while I am a fire sign I embrace the sacred
element of water.

These are the origins of my name
and who is Hortencia?
She is a guerrera,
una luchadora
que toda la vida ha tenido que luchar
para salir adelante
Hortencia does not give up easily
discouraged, yes,
Chillona, yes,
but she persists,
she keeps pushing
no matter the odds and obstacles

She has an inner strength that comes from her
ancestors
always guiding her
she is a spiritual woman

Hortencia is resilient
If one door closes
she looks for another
and makes her way.

Hortencia is a go-getter,
a leader,
a tender yet roaring soul
who leads with love,
compassion,

integrity,
and always with truth,
vulnerability,
and yes, rawness too,
which oftentimes gets her hurt.

Hortencia is a mosaico
of a multiplicity of colors.
She is the rainbow.
Her queerness
that has been rejected by others,
but she chooses herself,
over and over again.

Each time someone turns their back on her,
every time someone hurts her,
she loves herself even more,
she chooses herself even more
roaringly and tenderly.

Hortencia is love.
She is a free, sovereign being
who has had the courage
to leave societal expectations
to live her truth,
her authentic self.

While she is still in the journey
of fully embracing her name
and loving her name,
she radically
and unapologetically
loves herself
and chooses herself
every day.

You don't have to love your name
to honor it
with your actions,
with your values,
by walking
and living
your truth.

Chingona

Strong, badass chingonas
uplift other chingonas.

Aquí no venimos pa' chingaderas.
We're not here to gossip,
compete,
or tear each other down.
We don't mess with envidia,
ni celos,
ni mal de ojo vibes.
That's not the energy we carry
nosotras somos pura buena vibra y fuego.

Chingona,

NO ONE is your coompetition.

Your only competition
es la versión de ti misma from yesterday.
La meta is to grow,
heal,
learn,
and thrive
in tu vida personal,
your goals,
tu educación,
y tu healing journey.

Don't believe the toxic BS
that there's no room at the mesa,
that you gotta shrink,
stay quiet,
Que calladita te ves más bonita

Nosotros sabemos alzar nuestra voz

We know better.
We were never meant to fit in
We were meant to lead and shine bright

There's room for all of us.
We rise juntas.
We clap loud when otra mujer shines.
We break generational cycles
con coraje y corazón.
We build comunidad,
not competencia.

Focus on your gifts,
tu calling,
tu propósito.
This world necesita
what only YOU can offer.

Keep shining.
Keep growing.
Keep showing up.

Your light no le quita nada a nadie
reminds them que ellas también pueden brillar
a lo contrario it reminds…
No olives es que eres una Chingona hoy y siempre!

Queer

I am unapologetically queer.

I use the word *queer*
because it is expansive,
because it is fluid,
because it refuses boxes and binaries
that were never made for me.

What was once used
to shame,
to police,
to judge and punish,
I reclaim.

I reclaim it
as defiance,
as rebellion,
as resistance,
as love.

Being queer is more than
sexual attraction,
more than desire.

It is choosing to love
radically,
beyond what is prescribed,
beyond what is considered acceptable,
beyond the narrow scripts
handed to us by patriarchy and cis-
heteronormativity.

Being queer is choosing
a loving, respectful relationship
with the father of my children.
It is choosing care over conflict,
communication over resentment,
peace over performance.

It is building a blended family
that challenges conventional notions
of what family is supposed to look like
even when others reject these models,
even when they say
"Eso no se hace así."

Because as a queer woman,
I know that love is bigger
than tradition,
bigger than respectability,
bigger than fear.

Love transcends
what is socially acceptable,
what is prescribed,
lo que se tiene que hacer.

Being queer is refusing
heteronormativity,
patriarchy,
and gender policing
disguised as morality.

It is choosing to love differently,
to exist differently.
To move through the world
with intention
and courage.

It is choosing radical authenticity
over respectability.
Vulnerability over el *qué dirán*.

We, queer folks,
are loving,
caring,
empathetic,
embracing.

We carry tenderness
as strength.
We lead with heart
Tenemos un corazón enorme.

I am a proud, unapologetic queer woman
who refuses to love,
to live,
to exist
within traditional paradigms.

I choose love
I choose myself.

It Takes More Than

It takes more than
a pretty face,
nice looks,
O palabras bonitas
para conquistar
a esta Diosa divina.

SECTION 4
I AM MY OWN HOME:
DIOSA DIVINA

I Am a Divine Life Force

I am a divine life force,
the life force that shines bright
and illuminates darkness.

I am the life force that has been oppressed.
I am the erotic, sensual, and sexual life force
that your tía, abuelita, mamá, primas,
and other women in your life have shamed.

Patriarchy wants you to dim your light,
to shut down,
to suppress your life force
because it knows just how powerful you are
when you embody it.

Your erotic, sensual, and sexual energy
is powerful as fuck.
Believe it.

When you step fully into your life force,
you become unstoppable.
You create art,
beauty,
love,
and joy.

You shine so brightly
that your light ignites transformation
not just in your own life,
but in the lives of those around you.

Your life force is sacred.
Your life force is beautiful.
Your life force is freedom.
Your life force is sovereignty.
Your life force is liberation.
Your life force is infinite

And this

this is exactly what the patriarchy doesn't want
It has shamed you all your life,
conditioned you
to suppress your erotic life force.

It is time you say
a la chingada con esas pendejadas
and embrace your erotic, sensual life force,
because it's needed.

You are powerful
and you can use your life force
to create beautiful gifts,
to create healing for the world

See
your erotic, sensual, and sexual life force
is meant to be embraced
first and foremost by you.

You get to decide
if you want to share it,
how you want to share it,
and who is invited
into this sacredness.

Powerful women
who embrace their erotic life force
are powerful
because we understand
that we cannot be tamed
by the patriarchy

We are powerful
beyond measure.

I Am

I am the moon
that shines bright in the darkness.

I am the rain
that purifies your spirit.

I am the fire
that lights your path.

I am the air
that wraps you
with tenderness and love.

Soy las estrellas,
that radiate and shine bright
in your journey.

I am a woman
fierce and tender.
I am the daughter
who grew up between borders,
who misses her *mamá*
y *hermanas en México.*

I am the loving, caring mother
who will sacrifice for her children
but will never abandon
her dreams and aspirations.

I am divine
I am perfectly imperfect
I am my best friend.
The advocate.
The leader.
La jefa de su vida.

Diosa

You are a goddess
Eres una diosa
You are the divine feminine power!
Eres una diosa
Nunca lo olvides

Mis Caderas No Mienten

Mis caderas no mienten.
They sway to the rhythm of life,
side to side,
little by little,
without rush
because this isn't a race.
It's a sacred journey.

Erotic Embodiment is Divine Life Force

Erotic embodiment is divine life force that allows
the freedom to connect with my body
to honor any part of me that feels good, alive, and
present.

It is the gentle act of caressing my skin,
touching my face,
running my hands through my hair,
holding my arms,
feeling the strength of my legs.

Erotic embodiment is not only about sex.
It can be sensual.
It can be tender.
It can be simply noticing where pleasure lives in
my body,
and letting it guide me back to myself,
back to my wholeness.

Erotic embodiment is divine because it reminds us
we are not objects,
not bodies to be consumed.
We are sacred vessels,
creators of beauty and life,
bearers of knowledge, wisdom, and joy.

To embody the erotic
is to step into your own divine power,
to say *this body is not broken.*
This body is holy.
This body belongs to me.

Soy Una Mariposa

Soy una Mariposa,
a butterfly learning to spread her wings.

Once, I was a caterpillar,
caged in, suppressing my authenticity,
without knowing that one day,
I would break free,
dismantling the boxes
I was forced to live in.

La oruga, poco a poquito,
fue descubriendo que había más vida,
más libertad en el camino.
So she began the courageous journey of
transforming,
shedding,
releasing,
transmuting pain into something beautiful.

She was scared.
She was anxious.
Would she survive the journey?

And she did.

El dolor became beauty.
Soy mariposa con alas
que jamás dejará que nadie se las corte,
porque ha descubierto que
la mayor libertad es ser ella.

Vuela, mariposa.
Spread your wings, always.
Fly to horizons beyond imagination,
porque eres libre y hermosa

Love is a Woman

Love is a woman,
Not only a man.

To discover this has been
frightening
and beautiful.

We have been conditioned that there is one kind of
love.
A straight line.
A heteronormative love.
And to live that heteronormative script
Has left me wounded, in pain, and in grief.

Love does not know
binaries,
borders,
scripts,
or straight lines.

Love is simply love, regardless of social identities.
Un amor puro.
Un amor profundo.
Un amor hermoso.
Un amor sincero.
Un queer amor.

Yes, I have loved men.
But I also have loved women.
I am unapologetic about my love
and sexual attraction.

I am a mujer that is challenging binaries
que ama
con ternura,
con pasion,
con cariño.

A love for women that is
fierce,
passionate,
caring, and
gentle

En el Amor Todo Cambia y Todo se Transforma

En el amor todo cambia
y todo se transforma
A tu alrededor
En la manera que miras la vida
In how you see life and others

En el amor todo cambia
y todo se transforma
Como algo mágico
y hermoso
Y a veces también como
Duelo, oscuridad, y dolor
darkness and pain

En el amor todo cambia
y todo se transforma
No es bueno ni malo
It's not good or bad,
it just is.

En el amor todo cambia
y todo se transforma
Te puedes transformar
in the best
and highest version of yourself
O te puedes transformar en la peor versión de ti
Tu decides, you decide how love changes and
transforms it all

Being Alone

Being alone can be liberating,
it can be growth,
it can be exactly what you need
to reconnect with yourself.
And from that place of personal fullness,
you'll learn to choose someone from love,
not from need.

We live in a society
that obsesses over romantic relationships,
one that tells you something is wrong with you
if you're alone.

Being alone is a choice you are making
and you are not truly alone,
because you have yourself.

Being alone gives you the opportunity
to heal,
to reconnect with your spirit,
to tend to past versions of yourself,
and to honor the wounds
of your inner child.

You don't need someone to make you happy
because you embody happiness.
You radiate joy.
You are successful.
You are love.

Whoever comes into your life
will stand beside you
because you choose them
from a place of abundance,
not scarcity.

You choose who you allow
into your divine life
and energetic portal.
You are whole.

You don't need this person to fulfill you,
you are already fulfilled.
You don't need them.
You want them.
And that is the difference.

Being alone gives you clarity
about who you are.
It grounds you.
It strengthens your standards
and expectations.

You are not "too much,"
and you are not asking for too much.
You are simply a bad bitch
who has done the healing
to become this version of yourself.

And I know culturally
this is not easy.
La familia expects you
to "estar con alguien,"
because they've been taught
that happiness is tied
to being partnered.
But you know better.

You are breaking the chains.
You are showing your family,
your friends,
your children,
and anyone witnessing you
that you would rather be alone
than live a life
without purpose,
without meaning,
or without love
just to avoid
el qué dirán.

How many people do you know
who stay in relationships without love?
Por costumbre.
Por los hijos.
Por razones económicas.
Por miedo.
Por el qué dirán.
Por mil razones.
Many don't have the courage
to choose differently
or have the freedom to leave
and yet here you are,
doing the hard thing.
Choosing yourself.

You are not alone.
You have you
And that is powerful

Child-Free Latina

While I am not a child-free Latina,
I want to honor all who are.

In a world that blames women
for every choice we make
for wanting children,
for not wanting them,
for daring to choose ourselves
I see you.

Our society cuts programs
that support women,
then shames us
for the lives we build
outside of motherhood.

Who gets to be a mother?
Who decides what womanhood should look like?

To choose not to have children,
is not a failure.
It is not selfishness.
It is sovereignty.

Many mujeres
are pursuing education,
careers,
dreams that light their spirit
without needing to birth a child
to feel complete.

We were socialized to believe
our highest calling
was motherhood,
that fulfillment comes only
from cradling another life,
But that is a lie
passed down by patriarchy,
by culture,
by fear.

Becoming a mother
is a choice,
not an obligation.

Your worth does not bloom
from your womb.
It already lives
in your breath,
your brilliance,
your becoming.

Merezco

Me merezco el sol,
la luna,
y las estrellas.

Merezco que me traten
como la Diosa que soy,
como la dama que soy,
como la mujer completa
que siempre he sido.

Merezco ser escuchada
cuando mi voz tiembla,
ser vista
cuando el mundo me quiere invisible.

Merezco ocupar espacio
con mi cuerpo,
mi historia,
mi poder,
mi verdad.

Porque he llorado mares
y florecido en desiertos,
he sobrevivido tormentas
y aún así,
sigo brillando.

Me merezco el sol,
la luna,
y las estrellas
porque dentro de mí
habita el universo entero

Your Light

You don't need to justify your existence.
You don't need to explain your purpose.

Keep creating.
Keep rising.
Keep shining so damn bright
because your light
was never meant to be dimmed.
You were born to roar,
to remind the world
of your brilliance.

Come to Me

Don't come to me with empty words,
que se las lleva el viento.

Don't come to me with empty promises
hiding behind a mask,
pretending to be
what you are not.

Come to me heart-centered,
intentional,
raw,
vulnerable,
authentic

Come with your soul unveiled.
I can see and feel.
Come with your nakedness of spirit.
Come to me
as you are.

No Estás Sola

No estás sola.
Tus ancestros caminan contigo.
Your ancestors have your back,
Siempre.

You move through the world
with every single one of your ancestors.
Their breath in your lungs,
their prayers in your steps,
their love in your heart,
their DNA in your cells.

You are never alone,
even in your darkest and saddest moments.
Your ancestors hold you with love and tenderness.
They cleanse your tears
and whisper softly,
You live with the spirit of your ancestors.
You are them.

You have a lineage
of strength,
of resilience,
of joy,
of ancestral knowledge
wrapping your being
with a sacred rebozo
con amor y ternura.

Your ancestors hold you.
They carry you
on heavy
and gloomy days.

They whisper
No estás sola,
Siempre estamos contigo.

Chillona, y Bien Chingona

Chillona.
Sí.
Soy una chillona unapologetic.

What others call weakness,
I call strength.

The courage to feel out loud,
to let my heart speak
without asking permission.

Being chillona is vulnerability.
Es suavidad.
Es sentir profundamente.
Es tener un corazón enorme,
capaz de amar sin miedo,
de doler sin esconderse.

Do not confuse this with fragility.

Soy chillona y chingona.
Las chillonas son fieras.
Resilientes.
We overcome obstacles,
no nos rendimos,
no nos rajamos.
I was judged for my tears.
Told to "be a big girl,"
"a grown woman"
as if growing up meant drying out
not feeling, not crying
Nah, soy una chillona unapologetic!

I am a chillona
and I still cry por cualquier cosa.
Porque las chillonas
no tienen miedo de expresarse.

I cry for my ancestors
who couldn't cry,
who didn't know how to cry,
who had to swallow their emotions
to survive.

I cry for my current family members
who don't know how to cry
because trauma taught them silence.

I cry for the ancestors
in both of my lineages
especially the mujeres,
the ones who came before
and the ones still living.

Chillo en homenaje por ellas.
Chillo por alegría,
por tristeza,
por duelo,
por coraje.

Chillo porque siento.
Porque estoy viva.
Soy chillona unapologetic.

My tears
mis lágrimas chillonas
are a weapon of decolonization.
They are courage.
They are strength.
They are medicine.

Chillonas,

do not let anyone's judgment
dim your beautiful heart
or dull your sparkle.

Your tears heal ancestors
and future generations

Let them talk.
Let them shame.

At the end of the day,
they are threatened
by your vulnerability,
by your ability to lower your guard
and feel without armor.
That takes courage.
Y no todos pueden hacerlo.

Así que no lo olvides que
eres una chillona
bien
chingona!

Sueño

Sueño con un mundo
donde las mujeres
podamos existir completas
sin fragmentarnos
para caber,
sin ser encasilladas
en moldes o estereotipos que no son nuestros,
sin silenciar nuestras voces
para ser aceptadas.

Un mundo donde seamos
respetadas,
honradas,
y amadas
en todas nuestras dimensiones
la suave,
la fuerte,
la que ríe,
la que tiembla,
la que arde,
la que sana

Sueño y rambién sé
que ese mundo
lo estamos construyendo
Nosotras

Birthing

Birthing is not only what happens in a womb,
not only a path reserved for those
who can or choose to become mothers.

What, then, of the ones
whose bodies cannot carry children?
What of the women, the femmes,
the chingonas who choose themselves,
who choose to be childfree,
who choose a different way of creating life?

We are all birthing
every day, in the quiet ways no one sees.
Birthing when we release,
what no longer serves our spirit.
Birthing when we transmute pain
into language, into art, into breath.

Birthing when we shed the wounds
our ancestors carried so we don't have to.
Birthing when we renew ourselves
with intention, courage, and trembling hands.
Birthing is the ceremony of becoming

again and again,
with or without children,
with or without permission,
with or without a womb.

Because creation lives in us
in our grief, in our joy,
in every version of who we once were
and who we dare to become.

Biography

Dra. Hortencia Jiménez is a queer Mexican immigrant of Wixárika ancestry, born in the Sierra Madre in the state of Nayarit, Mexico. She is a sociology professor, author, health coach, podcaster, and mamá of three teenagers. She fell in love with reading at an early age and learned to read and write in English by typing passages from the books she loved, an experience that helped her become a fast typist and a lifelong reader.

Raised in an immigrant, working-class household by two single women who deeply valued education, though mentorship was limited, school quickly became her refuge and her path to possibility. She is a proud product of the public education system.

Dra. Jiménez earned her BA and MA in Sociology from San José State University and her PhD in Sociology from the University of Texas at Austin, where she also completed three graduate portfolios. She is a certified health coach who practices a non-diet, social-justice-centered approach.

An award-winning sociology professor, Dr. Jiménez is the author of *Challenging Inequalities: Readings in Race, Ethnicity, and Immigration* and co-author of Latinx Experiences: Interdisciplinary Perspectives, published by SAGE. Her research has appeared in multiple academic journals and has earned numerous recognitions within the Latine community.

Her work has been featured in media outlets including The Luz Media, BELatina News, Hip Latina, Poderositas, Hispanic Kitchen, and CanvasRebel Magazine. She has shared her expertise on radio and podcasts across the United States, including serving as co-host of *Comunidad en Contexto* on Joya 1570 AM. She has also presented at prestigious universities such as Stanford and Harvard, as well as at numerous community colleges and state universities.

Her podcast, *Dismantling Diet Culture: Fck* Being Calladita*, was ranked among the top three anti-diet podcasts in the nation in 2024. Through her scholarship, creative work, and coaching, Dra. Jiménez centers social and racial justice, empowering Latinx communities to heal their relationships with food, body image, and generational narratives.

When she's not teaching, reading, or writing, you can find her at the gym, cooking, tending her garden, and spending time with her three teenagers and her German Shepherd, Sol. Dra. Jiménez is a proud resident of Salinas, California, in Monterey County.

Acknowledgements

First and foremost, I want to thank Davina Agudelo, CEO and Founder of Alegría Media & Publishing, for believing in me and in the vision of this poetry collection. Davina, thank you for guiding me through this journey, my very first poetry book. Thank you for creating a safe space for my writing, for affirming my voice, holding space for my tears, and uplifting me every step of the way.

Thank you to Carlos Mendoza, graphic designer for Alegría Publishing. I deeply appreciate the care and intention you brought to the book cover and the layout of the poems. Gracias de corazón por tu paciencia y por honrar cada paso de este libro de poesía.

Special gratitude to Soni for believing in my vision and saying yes to designing the cover. Te aprecio muchísimo, amiga. I have immense respect and admiration for your art, and I feel so honored to have worked with you, not once, but twice. Thank you for capturing my vision, my sentiment, and my love so beautifully. I love this cover with all my heart.

Thank you, Yosimar Reyes for agreeing to write the foreword to my poetry book. It is truly a dream come true to have your words and message in these pages. Just like many people have their favorite musicians, you are one of my favorite poets. Soy una de tus fans, no solo por tu talento como poeta, sino por el gran ser humano que eres. You embody queer love, joy, resilience, tenacity, strength, and brilliance, plain badass!! Words fall short in expressing the gratitude I feel for your support, your belief in my work, and for lending your voice to this book. Gracias de corazón.

Thank you to the Hartnell College Foundation, Jackie Cruz, Kristine Edmunds, and Celeste De-Wald. Thank you for believing in my vision and for helping make it possible to create the Mariposa Rising Scholarship Fund, an endowed scholarship that supports undocumented students as they transfer to the university. Thank you for being part of this work rooted in community, art, healing, and legacy.

Thank you to Dr. Rahmatu Kassimu for supporting me in the final stages of this collection, helping me shape the manuscript, refine its structure, and bring clarity to its flow while creating a safe and affirming space for me.

Thank you to my therapist, Jasey, for creating a space where I could show up unfiltered, raw, and messily human. So much of this poetry was born from our session pláticas, conversations where truth, vulnerability, and healing were allowed to coexist. I will forever be grateful to have you as part of my healing journey. Thank you for honoring me as a queer woman of color. You have been, and will always be, an extraordinary therapist.

I want to thank my family for their love and support.

To my sister Patricia, thank you for modeling strength and resilience in every season of our lives. To my sisters Norma, Mayra, and Eva, aunque la frontera nos separa, siempre las llevo en mi corazón. Gracias por tanto amor, por sus oraciones, y por amarme y aceptarme. Las amo muchísimo y me siento muy orgullosa de ser su hermana.

Gracias, Mamá, por sus rezos, sus oraciones y su amor infinito que me sigue guiando y protegiendo. Sus oraciones de madre no conocen fronteras. Me siento profundamente orgullosa de tener una mamá con tanta fortaleza, sabiduría, alegría, inteligencia y talento. Tal vez no heredé su voz para cantar, pero llevo su legado artístico: usted como cantante y compositora, y yo como escritora. La amo, mamá.

Tío Elizar y Tía Florentina, los quiero muchísimo. Gracias por su amor, apoyo incondicional y por quererme y aceptarme en cada faceta de mi vida. Siempre estaré agradecida con ustedes.

To my cousins Jerry, Jr., and Dany, who are like brothers to me, thank you for your unconditional love, laughter, and support.

To Luis Jr., thank you for walking beside me with loyalty y corazón for so many years. I wish you deep, abundant happiness and success.

I also want to extend my deepest gratitude to my close friends, mentors, and the spiritual guides and medicine women who have walked with me throughout this creative process and across the different seasons of my life: Claudia C., Elizabeth R., Bianca E., Yoshiko M.A., Alicia E., Oliva M., Nancy (Lupita), Jeanette S., Lily A., Normita P., Laura O., Tina E., Yvy M., Alyssa A., Yanira H., Naz M., Getting to the Root, Cat Del Carmen, Rita Soledad F., Jessica R., Victoria L. and Cindy C. Your mentorship, medicine, presence, wisdom, amor, and prayers have carried me in more ways than words can express.

Special thanks to my gym bestie and fellow gym rat, Claudia Karina Trejo, for always motivating me to push heavier and believe in my strength and potential. Thank you for holding me with love during some of my most difficult moments as a mother and for your constant encouragement. Te aprecio mucho, amiga.

To all my gym friends, you know who you are, thank you for your friendship and motivation. Thank you for not judging my tears, for allowing me to exist as I am, and for holding space for both the cries and the gritos without judgment. So much of this energy was released from my body and transmuted into art, poetry, and love for humanity. Many of these poems were born in the lifting and in the crying.

Lastly, I thank my children: Luis, Itzel, and Elena, for being exactly who you are. Creator blessed me with the most precious gifts in this lifetime. I love you to the moon and back. My love for you is infinite, and I am endlessly proud and honored to be your mamá. Thank you for loving me, for your unconditional acceptance, and for honoring your queer mamá with such tenderness.

I dedicate this book to you. May you continue to live authentically and honor yourselves along the way. May our ancestors guide you, protect you, and bless you with wisdom, resilience, clarity, and discernment. Remember that you are never alone. You come from a strong lineage.

Con todo mi amor y gratitud
Hortencia Jiménez